BLUES TRIUMPHANT

Kevin—

Thanks for supporting this work.

In Triumph!

Jontavious Hadson

Blues
TRIUMPHANT

Jonterri Gadson

YesYes Books *Portland*

First Edition, 2016
ISBN 978-1-936919-37-6
Printed in the United States Of America

Published by YesYes Books
4904 NE 29th Ave
Portland, OR 97211
yesyesbooks.com

KMA Sullivan, Publisher
Stevie Edwards, Senior Editor, Book Development
Jill Kolongowski, Managing Editor
Alban Fischer, Graphic Designer
jamie mortara, Web Design and Management
Beyza Ozer, Deputy Director of Social Media
Amber Rambharose, Creative Director of Social Media
Phillip B. Williams, Coeditor In Chief, Vinyl
Mark Derks, Fiction Editor, Vinyl
JoAnn Balingit, Assistant Editor
Mary Catherine Curley, Assistant Editor
Johnna C. Gurgel, Assistant Editor, Publicity
Lewis Mundt, Assistant Editor
Carly Schweppe, Assistant Editor, Vinyl
Hari Ziyad, Assistant Editor, Vinyl
Cole Hildebrand, Intern

CONTENTS

RAPTURE

On a Saturday morning in Palm Beach,
middle-aged poets read stanzas of grief.
Now I know it will always be too soon
for my mother to die. It will happen
too slow, if not sudden. She might forget
me first, might not see her own face in mine
anymore, might sniff chamomile teabags
and not remember the evening we sat
at the dining room table, her bible
open to its index, finger pacing
over thin pages to find the perfect
verse to help me understand that vengeance
against boys who didn't call was the Lord's.
How we laughed, that day, at the wrath of God!

How we laughed, that day, at the wrath of God
blazing through Idaho's unbridled sun,
which baked me into a deeper darkness
but singed all the white girls red at church camp.
In days, their skin would simply peel and flake,
they'd molt into pretty bronze goddesses
with waves of blonde or brunette hair draping
their shoulders like Greek gowns. I watched the boys
stare at the Christian girls' exposed bellies
in cute contraband two-piece swimming suits,
their gazes snapped when counselors forced t-shirts
over girls' heads. Giggling under chilled sheets
in bunk beds pushed against cabin walls,
we dealt out boys' last names like playing cards.

We dealt out boys' last names like playing cards,
but I faked a soft snore before my turn,
offered myself as a sleeping martyr
so negotiations on forest hike
companions and bonfire first kisses
could go on without consideration
of race. Soon the moon cut through the windows
in square beams, framing our budding bodies
in cells of light, caging us like the camp's
promise that we'd all be saved by summer's
end, readied for the Rapture, born again
and available for pickup at noon
in the lot; only one of us desperate
to return to mother's gentle darkness.

To return to mother's gentle darkness,
to watch it unfurl, then feel it engulf,
to be hugged by that welcoming shadow
woman on a dry August afternoon
just two weeks before the first day of school,
to nuzzle against her warm, black comfort,
to be locked in a multi-toned brown-skinned
swirl, sway to the synchronized lullaby
of your deeps sighs, is to find home again
and believe that you won't have to leave it
for a cold schoolroom with vomit-colored
square tiles, where cute boys with mullets mutter
Communist when you enter the first time:
a biracial girl laughs hardest, loudest.

A biracial girl laughs hardest, loudest,
bunches her brow in quiet confusion
since they hadn't studied communism
in school yet. A yellow Polo sweater
gleams in the sun by the window, worn
by a tall girl whose relaxed hair slicks back
into one pristine black pigtail. A smile
lifts her ebony cheeks, then she exhales,
expels a deep, welcoming, warming sigh
to her automatic newfound best friend.
At recess they'd label us Pepper Girls.
I'd lie to my cousin, convincing him
they all chanted because we ran so fast,
saving him from knowing blackness mattered.

Saving him from knowing blackness mattered,
I whispered to Jimmy that I liked him
too. I sat in the desk behind him when
he scrawled notes in his margins in fifth grade
alphabet/number code that proved he loved
me. The repeated shush of paper torn
by vigorous, pre-pubescent boy hands
in denial ripped through the silent
classroom like quick flashes of white lightning
striking us — the unlucky, the exposed.
I saw Jimmy in the pool that summer
warning his cousins my black would come off.
You hoped so, Jimmy. I know you hoped so.

You hoped so, Jimmy. I know I hoped so
too. My body was tired of pushing
through water's resistance. If I'd been born
as a raindrop, I would have lost myself
upon impact with our deep, city pool;
I could have blended in and connected,
could have become unrecognizable
in its inseparable flow, survival
depending upon my ability
to diffuse. Or maybe I'd be soaked up
in a swimsuit; be folded, packed, and flown
to the coast; be worn again and wrung out.
Maybe, still, some part of me would wash up
on a Saturday morning in Palm Beach.

ON A
SATURDAY MORNING
IN PALM BEACH

GEOGRAPHIES OF DESIRE

Say God sat atop his first freshly-sculpted
      polar ice cap, crooning
            across oceans, wanting to reconcile
with the woman he left
      in the tropics, the woman who still loves him.
            How he misses his sun/her body,
returns to her as if lured
      by forces other than his own,
            thaws in her mouth, her navel,
in the grip of her sure hands,
      loses recollection of what she has to do
            with want or need, creates another
opposite end of the earth to run to,
      from the woman who still loves him
            who cries, *Why, God? Return to me*
and he, remembering his mercy, remains silent.

HOW WE LAUGHED, THAT DAY, AT THE WRATH OF GOD

DEFINE: MOTHER

If Jesus had grown tired
of other people's sins
the multiplying
being the miracle
his body bread
all of the tug
tug tugging at his hems

CARDINAL SIN

I don't love my son
the way I thought
my mother should love me

so I handed him a shoe box
to put the dead bird in
and shut the door.

It was a mistake,
not to be sure he buried it,
not to grab the children

gathered at my back door
by their shoulders
to push them into a half-circle

and a prayer.
Should have made them
take turns digging the hole,

each one of their pudgy hands
fingering stiff red's box
to lower it to the ground.

It wasn't my place
to teach other women's children
about death, so my own son

snuck the shoe box
into his backpack,
dead-eyed bird rolling

like a plastic prize ball,
told the principal
this cold puff

of field bird
had been his pet.
See him

clutching a coffin
the size of his feet,
eyes wide over a pout,

giving a man a reason
good enough to hold him. .

after Louise Glück

VIRGINIA BAPTIST

Prayer in a children's psych ward

Blessed sheets, sterile & foreign,
wrinkled over my child as he sleeps,
promise to warm him at least
to the temperature of my blood.
Holy bed, twin & tiny, teach me
how to be firm with his body,
but to yield for his spirit,
give me something to carry home
long after morning when he's risen,
once you've sprung back and forgotten
his shape, his weight
how much to give to hold him.

PATRICIDE EPISTLE

I.

I want to say we met like white space
meets blue sky in crayon drawings,
that we made a traceable line

over a chimneyed house
with two windows, stick figures
of my mother and I holding fingerless hands
beneath a tree, the sun in the corner

smiling; but few houses dot the dirty hills
of Albuquerque's bloodless skyline. Traffic
and traffic lights, stray cats and shattered glass
in guttered streets, you and me

not holding hands at the bottom
of the handicapped access ramp
leading into Long John Silver's.

I'm fourteen. You mispronounce
my name, stress the wrong syllable.

I don't call you dad, can't use your first name,
so I wait to be noticed. Hey you —

let's watch the sky purple and drain
between desert hills, from here,
where we can't tell
if the road ends or rises.

GLOSSARY OF
SELECTED TERMS

What is *skin*,
if not a taut swaddle

loosening, *body*
if not a warm swaddle

cooling, *blood*
if not thread

in a swaddle
made of body, *horizons*

if not lines
where sky swaddles

Earth. See *father*.
Stars, if not swaddled

matter emitting light. See *spirit*.
Wind, if it does not trace

paths around bodies. See *blood*.
Universe, if not outermost

concentric circle. See *mother*.
A *kiss,* if not mouths pressed

into wet twists, *taste*
if not flavor swaddling

tongue, *father*
if not the option

to swaddle, *spirit*
if not the smallest unit

of the swaddled, *mother*
if not hips

swaddling womb. See *skin*.
See *body*. See *wind.* See *universe*. See *blood*.

after Nin Andrews

BLUES TRIUMPHANT

I am a medley of waterfalls,
their loud shush.

I am a forgotten porch dog,
not the mutt
but his memories.

I am hidden in a secret
crease, a penny
pressed down under.

I am a bullet's hole
singing a wound song
into blood.

I am grief
rising between widows'
peaks.

I am rain
and the scent
of rain.

I am the fisherman's
surprise and the marlin
who hooks back.

I am the thrust
that left lovers
spent. I am the

Oh, God!
of their apex.

WE DEALT OUT
BOYS' LAST NAMES
LIKE PLAYING CARDS

INSTRUCTIONS FOR STAYING OUT ALL NIGHT

Stand in the Chevy's headlights,
talk to guys overdue for graduation

like you aren't a virgin after curfew
sucking beer from frozen Keystones.

When a muck slick Idaho boy shivers
shirtless toward you, let him heave

his breathless report of how fast
the forbidden irrigation slide shot him

dirty, into dark water. Blow stale breath
in country cops' faces, watch the orange tide

sunrise bubble up between the valley's open thighs
from the backseat of a cruiser. But first, fever

when your fingers bump his dripping hand
threatening to burst at its lifeline in the cooler

before his cold wet body
must dance back into blue jeans.

for Amy

ODE TO A MICROPHONE

This is about singing into a brush
with synthetic hair tangled in its bristles
in front of a spit-spotted mirror in a bathroom
where every song is your song and roaches
breakdance in slow motion when they're caught
in the blink and the buzz of the dying
fluorescent light while your hand wriggles electric,
trying to brush, gargle, and rinse in the click
and the three-second pause while the CD player
shuffles to the next disc. Do it all wet and naked
if this is about a broken broom stick, the handle
of a ratty mop, an unwrapped tampon, a remote control,
a black tennis shoe, an ink pen, a wire hanger, a dead light
bulb, a can of mousse, a freshly shaven bald head, my fist,
your fist, or anyone's.

WOMAN, FLUX

Night birds
know nothing
of me

in my lone bed
making lists
of things
I cannot change.

Let me be
a harmonious interruption

of hair and eyes,
skin, voice, and darkness,

my body
an intermittent flash
of starlight

that, at least,
from a distance
appears constant.

AN APPEAL

i.

Made of my body
a prison —

blood-smothered fetus
locked   between hollow
of breakable bone

this new body
sunk deep enough
to find comfort

in the reservoir
of my abandoned heat

ii.

Make justice
of my body—

soft walls begging enter
break me down, enter

when my stone hold slips open enter
your body listening

when my body asks
show it you want to come home.

TO RETURN TO MOTHER'S GENTLE DARKNESS

FINDING IDAHO

Your first mistake is believing
every aerial photo of anywhere
shows the roll of sagebrush
over the singed desert valley —
symptoms of a slow-setting sun.

Eyes that never leave a mother's
windows believe they've found home
in the first cluster of roofs in a cul-de-sac,

believe they know each troubling pass —
how steep, how thin, how rocky,
where the road has no railing,
the exact spot where you learned to yield.

MERCY

When the sow doesn't refuse them her sequence of teats.
When her swollen spotted body, bristles spearing mud

permits a dozen snouts burrowing beneath her —
unapologetic litter of grunts, hungry self-serving soldiers,
cacophonous squeals urging over, over.

Not to protect her face from their hooves,
but that she could crush them, we pen her in. Narrow.
Leave only enough room for her to lay down.

When she doesn't, in a quiet rage, slaughter them herself
she suffers each unrelenting mouth, she sates our wild
    expectations.

MOTHER

This woman needs to be held
to hold.

I still crave the quivering steam cloak
that rises between close bodies

still want to christen my lover
where sweat pools in my back's dip

still make enough heat to twist tongues
dry in my open mouth

to leave sprawling limbs
veining white sheets

bare bough reaching.

GIRL, 11

A mouth is a sideways woman,
her curves and dips, the way she opens,
how her hollow center can sing.

Mother, your mouth
is a fallen cello,

your husband's hands—
a casket. Full of me.

CONSUMMATION

Everything parents us:
looming shade trees
with people names,
each granule of sand
with its own heartbeat
lives to give the sensation
of kiss. We are the light
all green grows toward.
Everything touched
touches back.

COMPENSATION

If He-Man had been raised
by a single mother,
there might've been times
when she'd catch him
holding his hands as if to protect
a freshly-painted set of fingernails
or pursing his lips tight enough to spit
when he'd sass her, I mean, one hand
on the hip opposite his sheath sass her.
I know about her vow
to be more like a man for him,
how it was then she decided
his would be the mightiest sword.

WHEN A BOY KISSES YOUR SON

Remember you used to kiss girls
how you played boyfriend
and girlfriend with no boys

just your hipless day-of-the-week
panties pressed together in the top bunk
grinding to shivering warmth

how it shook you like morning's first stretch.

DRIVING AWAY FROM THE CHILDREN'S PSYCH WARD

Though sunrise presses
against your eyes
commits itself

to memory, asphalt
lit in its violent light,
leaves turning
shame-faced in the wind,

best to begin accepting
neither this mile marker nor that
can track your nonexistent distance

from what you had to leave behind
from what is coming toward you
for you, yes, even still.

WE WHO BITE
THE HAND

The asses that sit on grocery story eggs
        praying they will hatch belong to

the hands that sever worms and snap
        beetle's backs just so we can build a bug hospital

with the same fingers that pick our own scabs
        until dots of blood rise up

to suck away with hot mouths
        full of thick tongues we have yet to grow into,

        our gums — corridors for exposure of bones
otherwise kept secret, smuggled in blood, our bodies

        crossing borders committing punishable offenses.
Children, what are we, if not interruptions?

        Our bodies impermanent tattoos on the air's broad back.
Nothing to stop us from believing

        even the space after a colon is meant for us.

PATRICIDE EPISTLE

II.

The first time I had you killed
I made you a hero of the Vietnam War.
The third grade social studies textbook said
young foreign boys hid grenades
during corner games, seamstresses doubled
as spies. Why wouldn't you have died
on those streets, clutching my mother's
photo with your thumb pressed cold
against her belly, wishing you'd had a chance
to propose, hoping for a girl? But that war
ended before I was born. Next,
I had a drunk driver end you. Said I visited him
in prison to spit in his face. Forgave him
for a speech during health class. In eighth grade,
I made you die young of natural causes,
so I could teach a grieving classmate
the proper way to mourn.

A BIRACIAL GIRL LAUGHS HARDEST, LOUDEST

A FOSTER
MOTHER'S CHILD

Smeared coffee-rings stained the outside of the manila folders that arrived an hour or two before the State of Idaho placed its freckled unfortunate in my mother's house. They'd come with one half-empty box of the broken things they were allowed to remember—a hand-painted porcelain piggy bank with the coin slot chipped into a belly gorge, a naked blonde Barbie with no arms and a buzz-cut, a pasted four-leaf clover. The kind of luck they needed couldn't be crafted with a glue stick. Still, those little white kids wore their bruises like plastic gold dollar store sheriff's badges that gave them authority over any anguish in my mother's house. It was hard to complain when my temporary siblings had court documents falling out of a folder in the living room, documents declaring that C.J. staring at me in Earth Science was insignificant in comparison, even if C.J. had sparked the off-topic conversation that ended with his proclamation that his family would never approve of him bringing home a black girl. The cold ivory iron hearts of my daybed chilled my scalp where my auburn-streaked curls parted as I lay mum, more giddy than ashamed, replaying the moment in fifth period when I came the closest I had ever been to being liked by a boy.

WARD OF THE STATE

Pica makes her hungry
for my mother's walls.
She eats them, picks

down to the pink
fiberglass fur
at home center.

Skeleton frame
exposed, she leaves

piss rot
in the heat vents.

We smell her
while spooning
warm breakfasts,

madness spreading
all over our house
like it belongs to us.

IDAHO PRIMER

You don't know sin
        until you've been the black girl
                in the cab of a white boy's Chevy

parked outside a Circle K
        when his door shoves another white boy
                by mistake and their puffed chests circle

while you watch through the window,
        until the one you're with is ready
            to smash a push broom

over the other one's head
        . . . as soon as he's finished his monologue: *Dude,*
           I'm just trying to buy some condoms

and get some ass. Once he's pointed you out,
        once you smile and wave just your fingers
            as the rage drains from their faces

once they've shaken hands and you believe yourself
        common ground, a peace maker—that cute,
           without wondering what message

passed between their palms,

      only then can you begin to know

         how darkness deepened

beneath that slow-setting sun.

SYMPTOMS OF A SLOW-SETTING SUN

Think sagebrush rolling, no high-pitched
oo wee oo wee oooo, no gray Western flick,

real tumbleweed passes through high beams
on two lane roads, sticks in your wheel sockets.

This town cut in on the desert's dance
with forest-shawled mountains, left her laying sun-licked,
brush ablaze, bulldozed for paved roads, intersected.

Suffer a sleight of hand, a misplaced moment
of reflection and nearby cliffs will kill you.
Here, the sun is a woman's full breast,

tickled by tip-tops of evergreens,
this is her blushing sky. She's the light that saves
or maims you, depending on how bent she is to shine.

SAVING HIM FROM KNOWING BLACKNESS MATTERED

INSTRUCTIONS FOR LEAVING YOUR BODY

be the breath behind the air
>the breath that breathes it

be dark pupils
>bleeding like black ink past the edges of eye white

be shadow
>bending out of hands, knees

be spoon
>dipping into your own darkness

be only the metallic scent of rain

be echo
>alive in the pause after your own scream

be rupture

TO WOMEN WAITING FOR THE GYNECOLOGIST

Deep inside this cabin, deeper
still into the darkness
arising like fumes, like odor
of woman, broke, harnessed

in a body, by the bodies
of men who believe me
animal, wild, and numb
because my body be

black, be able, be stank after
childbirth, ruined cast out
into the woods to spoil alone.
My savior wears white coats

bends spoons, bends me, bends spoon
into my crouched hound of body.
White women rest easy in clean
sheets, while spoons scrape through me,

give me new hollows. He
will one day find, in me, how to
mold the tool, the pressure,
his, to relieve those precious as dew

drops settled on dove's wings
will be gone. And you, innocent
you, lying on cool white
slabs, free legs ready, no remnants

of me in you until
you are pressed wide open, coffee
brewing in the next room,
kind instruments probing you softly.

LILIES FOR
EDDIE KING, JR.

When all else in the landscape is green —
suddenly orange tiger lilies,
so much like a bedraggled Eddie King, Jr.

tearing open his trench coat
to reveal to the group that went on
singing without him

that he was still holding on
in the gold glitter jumpsuit
he'd performed in years ago.

If we could hear color refracting,
this bright patch of lily horns
would sing the sound Eddie had only his mouth to make —

not *TADA!* but *DAA-AA-AANNG!*
A man making his own echo,
a reverberation of his former self,

or maybe just a perfect replicator
of the cartoon sound light makes when it glints
off and away from brilliant objects at immeasurable speeds.

COUSINS

On the rock slide behind Building 10,
we crushed pebbles into powder
and plotted replacing what his mother smoked

with the products of our pounding.
Peanut butter breath and rubble dust hung
in the sliver of summer air between us.

His mini-fists gripped the sharp edges
of the broken stone mallet he drove
into his growing mound of grit that would always be

bigger than mine under the ferocious bang of a boy
whose whole body rocked to his determination
to smash the world as he knew it to pieces.

When the first big rock split open,
I looked at him and didn't breathe;
he looked at me, didn't breathe;

we looked at the center of a rock
for the first time, together,
expecting magic.

Some days I'll remember that day
as the day we realized, forever,
a rock is just a rock

through to its core. But when alcoholism
comes to him as naturally as his dimples,
this day will be an exhale; the final finger flex

of his throbbing fist; it will be blood
seeping from cut hands—all of the blood—
drops that dripped free and those that pooled

in his dirty palm to dry up together,
to waste, in the cracks in his lifeline.

YOU HOPED SO,
JIMMY. I KNOW
YOU HOPED SO.

ALL APOLOGIES

A rumor starts as a whisper,
a breathy message
from an omnipotent they.

They say Jimmy ran away.

Suppose you've just been given
a peppermint-scented secret
about a boy you probably would have loved
next week. It will sting
as if his turn had already come,
hurt like he'd been the one
to give you that unfamiliar
too sweet to be sweat wetness
in your flower-printed panties
just by looking you in the eye
today. You will want to be held,
want to grab the nearest neck
to drip *I loved him* in an ear.

You will want to be noticed.

When his body is found,
you'll drive to the coast
to link arms with his family

and set his ashes free
over fickle waves, only, the ocean
will refuse to hold him,
will blow bits of Jimmy back
in your face with a breeze
saltier than his father's tears.

In the distance, someone will mistake
the sound of your choking
on the ashes of a runaway as laughter.

PATRICIDE EPISTLE

III.

If you can't stand to hear your own voice
echo in the house since your mother died and left you
with no body to buffer sound,

turn the TV on when you leave for work,
let Oprah greet you while you unlace your boots
and rub your own feet after a long day.

Father, if you need me
I can teach you how to be lonely.

I will show you how to swaddle yourself
in a blanket that will warm your body
to the temperature of blood.

ON A
SATURDAY MORNING
IN PALM BEACH

CLING

We both grip the fountain's
damp lip, lose our knuckle tips

just beneath the water's surface,
our cheeks lift into simultaneous

hello smiles, while the ivy spreads
like fresh disease in the corner's shadow.

Had I known freedom
could matter so much,

I would have loosed the ivy's vines
from the cold stone hold

of that mildewing, chipped, brick
wall then, would have plucked

each leaf off above their stems
let the vines sprawl naked in the dirt

like earth's veins. I'd had enough
of watching the slightest changes ripple

our reflections unrecognizable.
You'd grown tired of the shade

shifting, had enough of trying.
Still, we walked out together

our wind rustling the evergreen ivy
that, unlike us, would lose nothing

for clinging, struggling to rise
toward an unreachable sun.

HOME IMPROVEMENT

Rust scars surviving colors
in Seattle's skyline, spreads as scabs

across red scrap metal, rots in speckles
over yellowing fences, blossoms

like bruises on a blue shed
in a backyard where he pummels
a cement patio to dust as a hobby.

Her face in the window reflects
wet ruin, counts each punished stone.

SYSTEM OF SYSTEMS

As tree, for lust of leaf, wavers in cold winds
branches into a darkening sky;
as homes shape horizons, so do I,
vein this space, this air, my unwieldy molecules
wild as morning hair. Blood roots
through body, body spines this bed
where we lay with our backs to one another
nothing between us but whispers, winding
through sound waves, atmospheric capillaries
carrying waste, trapped in cells, each their own body.

We are nucleus, rooted to fruitlessness, reaching
though shaking in the chill of this, our winter.

A BODY'S WINTER

Snow coats the next day's waking
after each of the sun's
most radiant offerings.

This can be explained.
As weather. Its patterns
of pressure. I know it only as want

breaking like long fever,
just to warm, sick again.

Reoccurring storms
make unnavigable countries
of foreign bodies. I ache

to be atmospheric; to hoard
the swirl, the dip of visible breath
through each of my livable layers.

FERAL WOMAN

No one has touched me for weeks
yet in this drugged, gilt afternoon, late,

when nothing is safe, I'm paralyzed
as though so wildly desired
— from "Midas Passional" by Lisa Russ-Spaar

finds herself
lost in thoughts of gold hairs
sprouting from another
woman's nape

as if they could be
rope enough
for reaching,

prays for lightning
from the highest point
of her wreckage,

considers suicide
with the unrelenting
press of sunlight
against her bare back,

though, even still, she cannot be
convinced of the necessity
of shadows.

She'd rather believe
in magic, in communing
with other disappeared things:

rabbits, women's torsos, rope snippings.

INHABITANTS

Now that March's scrambled sticks are June's cradle
in the corner of my rented house's porch, now

that I've witnessed the stretch of baby birds' necks
toward the drooped bug in their mother's peck of mouth,

now bees, now their hover nearer the hive they've built
under loose floorboards, now their hum, now striped

buzzing clouds, now that I've scoured and scraped
preparing for the prospective new tenant's parade, I know.

I never mean to be temporary.

LETTERS THAT WON'T
BE SENT EITHER

I.

Dear Maple Leaves Falling with Grace,

> You look like empty
> upturned hands
>
> catch her.

II.

Dear Dad Carrying His Daughter Like a Boombox,

> Her stomach goes
> girl girl girl girl
>
> Listen.

III.

Dear Bean Tombs,

> Does crisping hurt?
> Discarded scabs, wound lids,
> how does it feel

to be picked   to be picked   to be picked

over?

Dear Carcass Womb,

      Stillbirth is still birth.

Dear Pregnant Pod Bellies,

      Have you seen
      the bean tombs?

IV.

To all the men I've loved before:

Keep the poems.

IN MY RUSH

The first time I saw myself
reflected in well water,

I became light. Now no one knows
how to hold me. A valley is nothing

but the lowest point in the curve
of a woman's hip; a river — nothing —

if not her sway. Lightbearer translates
to Lucifer. I still want to be held. Hold me

like sound — in your throat,
with your breath, on your tongue.

I'll be a river on purpose.
We'll make a braid of our legs.

FORGET, FOR NOW

the hymn of wind through palm fronds,
the shuffle of fallen leaves on the lawn like dry hands
passing over one another again and again.

Forget diseased trunks, softened to splintering
strands, bugs cycling through, threatening
to sting if alarmed, spotted backs signaling danger.

How tempting to wish to be encased,
to have a hardened shell, to appear frightening enough
not to suffer the closeness that leads to harm.

ACKNOWLEDGMENTS

The poems in my chapbooks, *Interruptions* (Miel Books) and *Pepper Girl* (YesYes Books) are included in this manuscript.

Also:

"In My Rush," *Cream City Review*

"We Who Bite the Hand" and "Cousins," *The Rumpus*

"Woman, Flux," *Los Angeles Review*

"Mercy," "All Apologies," *Callaloo*

"An Appeal," "A Body's Winter," *The Collagist*

"System of Systems," *1110/4*

"Blues Triumphant," *Anti-*

"To Women Waiting at the Gynecologist," *TheThePoetry*

"Cardinal Sin" appears as "Cycle" in *Vinyl*

"Glossary of Selected Terms," *PANK* (print edition)

"Mother," *PANK* (online edition)

"Letters That Won't Be Sent Either," *Tidal Basin Review*

"Idaho Primer" and "Ward of the State," which appears as "Ward," *Poetry Quarterly*

"Patricide Epistle II" appears as "Horizons" in *Sugar House Review*

"Patricide" and "Instructions for Staying Out All Night," *Milk Money*

"When a Boy Kisses Your Son," *Muzzle Magazine*

"Compensation," *TORCH*

"A Foster Mother's Child," *Assisi*

"Ode to a Microphone," *Diverse Voices Quarterly*
"Rapture," *Conte*

Thanks to my Cave Canem family for the love, support, education, inspiration, fire, hugs, affirmations, and hoots and hollers that carried me and carry me still.

I am deeply grateful for the support I received through Dr. Charles Rowell's Callaloo Creative Writing Workshop and the transformative experience of working with Vievee Francis and Greg Pardlo.

Thank you to YesYes Books and KMA Sullivan for believing in me and my work. Thanks also to Miel Books and Éireann Lorsung, *The Rumpus* and Brian Spears for doing the same.

I would like to thank the University of Virginia's Creative Writing MFA program, its faculty, staff, and my poetry workshop mates for their feedback and support. Thank you to my thesis advisers Greg Orr, Rita Dove, and Lisa Russ-Spaar. Thanks to the faculty and staff of Drake University's English Department, the faculty and staff of University of Dayton's English Department for supporting me and my work as the Herbert W. Martin Creative Writing Fellow, the waiters, social staff, faculty, and contributors at Bread Loaf, and the Rockefeller Brothers Fund/Pocantico Center for the time and space to write.

To the faculty and staff of Bloomfield College's Humanities Division, thank you for providing the support I need to do the work I love with students and on the page.

Thanks to my blood family.

Thanks to my chica/cousin/sister, Chela Gage, my soulmate, Michelle Peñaloza, my girls, Sandrell Apatira and Quiana Lowe, my oldest friend Amy Lance and her mother, Donna Lance, to Metta Sáma for her love and support, to Lisa Fink and Zayne Turner for being close readers and great friends. Thanks, especially, to all the great therapists I've had.
And thanks, always, to Jabrien.

Jonterri Gadson is the author of the chapbooks, *Interruptions* (MIEL, 2014) and *Pepper Girl* (YesYes Books, 2012). She has received scholarships and fellowships from Cave Canem, Bread Loaf, University of Dayton and the University of Virginia where she received her MFA in Creative Writing. She is also a graduate of the Callaloo Creative Writing Workshop. Her poetry has appeared in *Callaloo, Los Angeles Review*, *The Collagist*, and other journals. She currently serves as Assistant Professor of Creative Writing/English at Bloomfield, College in New Jersey.

ALSO FROM
YESYES BOOKS

Full-Length Collections

i be, but I ain't by Aziza Barnes

Love the Stranger by Jay Deshpande

North of Order by Nicholas Gulig

I Don't Mind If You're Feeling Alone by Thomas Patrick Levy

If I Should Say I Have Hope by Lynn Melnick

Some Planet by jamie mortara

Boyishly by Tanya Olson

Pelican by Emily O'Neill

The Youngest Butcher in Illinois by Robert Ostrom

A New Language for Falling Out of Love by Meghan Privitello

American Barricade by Danniel Schoonebeek

The Anatomist by Taryn Schwilling

Panic Attack, USA by Nate Slawson

[insert] boy by Danez Smith

Man vs Sky by Corey Zeller

The Bones of Us by J. Bradley
    [Art by Adam Scott Mazer]

Frequencies: A Chapbook and Music Anthology, Volume 1
    [*Speaking American* by Bob Hicok,
    Lost July by Molly Gaudry
    & *Burn* by Phillip B. Williams
    Plus downloadable music files from
    Sharon Van Etten, Here We Go Magic, and Outlands]

Vinyl 45s
A Print Chapbook Series

After by Fatimah Asghar
Dream with a Glass Chamber by Aricka Foreman
Pepper Girl by Jonterri Gadson
Bad Star by Rebecca Hazelton
Still, the Shore by Keith Leonard
Please Don't Leave Me Scarlett Johansson by Thomas
    Patrick Levy
A History of Flamboyance by Justin Phillip Reed
No by Ocean Vuong

Companion Series

Inadequate Grave by Brandon Courtney

Poetry Shots
A Digital Chapbook Series

Nocturne Trio by Metta Sáma
    [Art by Mihret Dawit]
Toward What Is Awful by Dana Guthrie Martin
    [Art by Ghangbin Kim]
How to Survive a Hotel Fire by Angela Veronica Wong
    [Art by Megan Laurel]
The Blue Teratorn by Dorothea Lasky
    [Art by Kaori Mitsushima]
My Hologram Chamber Is Surrounded by Miles of Snow
    by Ben Mirov
    [Images by Eric Amling]